Easy Homemade Pizza Recipes -50 delicious pizza dishes to make at home-Cooking with Kids Series

by Debbie Madson

www.kids-cooking-activities.com

This homemade pizza cookbook doesn't just cover traditional pizza it goes beyond pizza with ideas such as pizza soup, Stromboli, pizza bubble bread, pizza cups and many more. Not to worry, we have some of our best traditional pizza crust recipes included in the cookbook as well.

But maybe you'd like a nontraditional pizza crust like zucchini crust or cauliflower crust? Whether you are teaching your kids to cook, or creating family meals, change up your pizza menus with these easy and fun recipes. There are enough meal ideas to last you almost a whole year of Friday pizza nights.

Thanks to some of www.kids-cooking-activities.com readers for contributing their favorite pizza recipes.

D1445752

Contents

Homemade Pizza Dough

Ingredients

1 T. or 1 pkg. Active dry yeast
1 Cup warm water
1/2 tsp. Salt
2 tsp. olive or canola oil
2 1/2-3 1/2 Cups flour
sprinkle cornmeal

Dissolve yeast in warm water. Let sit several minutes. In mixer, add salt, oil and 2 1/2 Cups flour. Stir in yeast mixture and slowly add just enough extra flour until dough clings to side of bowl and makes a ball. Knead about 5 minutes. Place in a greased bowl, cover and let rise until doubled about 1 hour.

Directions

Brush pizza pan with oil and sprinkle with cornmeal. Spread out pizza dough to all sides of the pan. Add sauce and toppings as desired. Bake at 450 degrees for about15-20 minutes until pizza is browned and cheese is melted.

Italian Pizza Dough

Ingredients
5 Cups flour
1 tsp. Salt
2 Cups warm water
2 T. yeast
1 T. Italian seasoning or mixed herbs
1 T. oil

Directions
Dissolve yeast in warm water. Let sit several minutes. In a food processor or mixer, mix together seasoning, flour and salt. Add in yeast mixture and continue to mix until dough starts to form a ball. Pour 1 Tablespoon oil while mixer is running. Place in an oiled large bowl and cover with a clean towel. Let rise 1 hour or until doubles in size. Grease pizza pan and prepare pizza as you'd like.
Cook at 450 degrees for 10-15 minutes until pizza is browned and cheese is melted.

Freezing Pizza Dough

Make next week's pizza dinner come together quicker by freezing a batch of pizza dough.

- Double your batch of pizza dough and freeze half the dough for another day. You can freeze the dough before rising, just add to a Ziploc bag and place in the freezer. Unthaw the night before by placing in the fridge.

- Another option for freezing pizza dough is to let the dough rise and then spread onto pizza pan. Flash freeze. Wrap pizza crust in plastic wrap and tin foil. Freeze until ready to use.

- You can also bake a plain pizza crust, allow to cool and wrap it in plastic wrap. Then freeze for another day.

Wheat Pizza Crust

Ingredients
2 1/4 Cups warm water
2 T. sugar
1 T. instant yeast
3 T. olive oil
2 tsp salt
2 Cups whole wheat flour
3 3/4 Cups bread flour

Directions
Add warm water and yeast together. Sprinkle the top with sugar and let sit several minutes. Meanwhile, add in a mixer flour, oil and salt. Slowly add in yeast mixture while mixer is running. Mix until dough forms a ball. Knead several minutes on a clean surface and place in an oiled large bowl. Let rise 30 minutes. Prepare crust in greased pizza pan.

This recipe makes enough for **three crusts** so you can prebake extras and allow to cool and freeze for another day.

To bake, place in a 400-degree oven for 20 minutes or until the cheese has melted.

Deep Dish Homemade Pizza

Ingredients
3 Cups flour
2 T. oil
2 eggs
1 Cup warm water
1 teaspoon salt
1 Tablespoon yeast
pinch of sugar

Directions
In small bowl add warm water, pinch of sugar and yeast. Set aside. In a mixer, add flour, salt, oil and eggs. Blend together several minutes. Pour yeast mixture in mixer while it is slowly running and mix several minutes until dough forms a ball. Knead dough 3-5 minutes. Place in a greased bowl and cover with a clean towel. Let rise for 1 hour. Separate dough into two balls and press into and up the edges of two circle pans. Then add your pizza sauce, shredded cheese and choice of toppings. Bake at 425 degrees for 20-30 minutes until golden brown and cheese is melted.

Pizza Pockets

Ingredients

2 T. vegetable oil
1 Cup flour
1/3 Cup milk
1 tsp. Baking powder
1/2 tsp. Salt
pizza sauce
pizza toppings
egg, for brushing the top

Directions

Place all ingredients into a mixer and beat until dough forms a ball. Take dough out of bowl and knead on a clean floured surface for several minutes. Cover with a clean towel for 15 minutes.

Roll dough into a large circle onto a flat cookie sheet or baking stone. Brush top of dough with oil. Spread half of the dough with pizza sauce and your choice of toppings leaving room along the sides. Fold empty half of dough onto half with toppings. Turn edges inwards and pinch together to seal. With a fork, prick top of dough in several places for the steam to come out. Beat an egg slightly and brush top of dough with beaten egg. Bake until golden brown about 20-25 minutes in a 425 degrees oven.

Pizza Stromboli

Ingredients
Using your favorite pizza dough recipe, roll dough into a rectangle.
In a small bowl, combine
2 egg yolks,
1 T. parmesan cheese
1 T. olive oil
1 T. parsley
1 T. oregano
sprinkle of pepper

Directions
Then sprinkle with desired toppings, such as shredded cheese and pepperoni. Roll up jelly roll style. Pinch seams to seal and tuck ends under. Place seam side down on a greased baking sheet. Brush the top with egg whites. Bake at 350 degrees for 35-40 minutes. Slice loaf and serve with warm pizza sauce.

Pizza Empanadas

Ingredients
1 1/2 Cup flour
1 Cup cornmeal
1 tsp. baking powder
1/4 tsp. salt
1 tsp. sugar
1/3 Cup butter, softened
1/2 Cup milk
1 Cup pizza sauce
1/2 Cup shredded cheese

Directions
Pre-heat oven to 400 degrees. In a mixer, add flour, cornmeal, baking powder, salt and sugar. Add in butter and combine until crumbly. Slowly stir in milk until dough forms a ball. If dough is too sticky, sprinkle in more cornmeal.

Place half of dough on a floured surface and roll dough out. Using a round cookie cutter or glass, cut dough into 3-4-inch circles. In small bowl, blend the sauce and cheese together. Add a spoonful of sauce mixture onto each circle. Fold circle in half and seal edges by pressing with a fork. Bake on an ungreased cookie sheet for 10-12 minutes until golden brown.

Easy Pepperoni Scrolls

Ingredients
1 lb. bread or pizza dough, frozen bag or batch of homemade dough
1 lb. sliced or chopped pepperoni
1 1/2 Cups shredded mozzarella cheese

Egg wash:
1 egg
1 T. water

Directions
Roll dough out into a large rectangle. Spread pepperoni and cheese over the top of the dough. Roll up the dough as you would cinnamon rolls. Press the ends together. Cut into slices with a knife and place on a cookie sheet. Brush each pizza scrolls with egg wash. Bake at 350 degrees for 25-30 minutes until golden brown.
Serve with pizza sauce on the side for dipping, if desired.

Pepperoni Bread

Ingredients
1 Cup + 2 T. warm water
1/3 Cup shredded mozzarella cheese
2 T. sugar
1 1/2 tsp. Garlic salt
1 1/2 tsp. dried oregano
3 1/4 Cups flour
1 1/2 tsp. Yeast
2/3 Cup pepperoni, chopped

Directions
In bread machine add all ingredients except pepperoni. Start cooking and just before the final kneading (your machine may audibly signal this) add the pepperoni.

If you don't have a bread machine, dissolve yeast in warm water. Sprinkle with sugar and set aside. In mixing bowl, add flour, oregano, garlic, pepperoni and cheese. Stir together and slowly add in yeast mixture. Beat until forms a ball of dough. Cover and let rise until doubles. Place in a greased loaf pan and bake at 350 degrees for about 20 minutes until golden brown.

Pepperoni Drop Biscuits

Ingredients
2 Cups biscuit/baking mix
3/4 Cups milk
3 T. butter melted
1/2 tsp. Garlic powder
1/2 tsp. Italian seasoning
3 1/2 oz. Pepperoni, chopped
2/3 Cup shredded cheddar cheese

Directions
In a mixing bowl, combine biscuit mix, milk, butter, garlic powder and Italian seasoning. Stir in pepperoni and shredded cheese. Mix all together until well combined. Drop by spoonfuls or scoops onto ungreased cookie sheet. Bake in a 400-degree oven for about 15 minutes or until golden brown.

Pizza Dough Pretzels

Ingredients

can pizza crust or batch of homemade
egg white
chopped pizza toppings such as finely chopped
pepperoni, shredded cheese, and/or garlic salt

Directions

Take small pieces of dough and roll into long ropes.
Make a loop with your rope and cross the top. Lay
strips dough over the top. Bake in a 350-degree oven
for about 10-15 minutes or until golden brown.

Bubble Pizza

Ingredients:
1 lb. ground beef
1-2 Cups pizza sauce
2 tubes refrigerator biscuits or pizza dough
1 1/2 Cups shredded mozzarella cheese
1 Cup shredded cheddar cheese

Directions:
Cook beef until brown and drain off grease. Mix sauce into beef and set aside. Cut biscuits or take small pieces of pizza dough and place in a greased 13 x9 casserole dish. Layer until bottom of dish is filled. Spread sauce beef mixture over the top of the bread. Bake in a 400 degrees oven for about 20 minutes. Add cheeses to the top and bake an additional 5-10 minutes until cheese is melted.

Quick Pizza Toast

A quick snack or dinner kids can easily prepare themselves with supervision.

Directions:

You can prepare this in a toaster oven or oven. Top a slice of bread with spaghetti or pizza sauce. Then sprinkle with shredded mozzarella cheese. Spread the top with pepperoni, ham or other pizza toppings you like. Broil in oven for 5-10 minutes until cheese melts.

Skillet Pizza
by Samantha (NY)

Ingredients
(1) *Flour or Multigrain tortilla (smaller than burrito size)
1/4 cup of tomato sauce or pizza sauce
1/4 tsp each, dried oregano and dried basil
1 tsp grated Parmesan
1/2 cup shredded low fat mozzarella
1/4 toppings of choice (optional) (ex. vegetables, turkey pepperoni, etc.)
Non-stick cooking spray olive oil flavor

Directions:
Spray non-stick pan with cooking spray. Place the naked tortilla in cold pan.
Spread sauce on top of tortilla and sprinkle with dried seasonings and Parmesan cheese.

Spread the mozzarella and add toppings on top of cheese. Turn the heat on for skillet to medium and allow the tortilla to toast in skillet until toasted on the bottom to the desired color and the cheese is melted.

Carefully slide the "pizza" onto a plate and let sit for 1 minute to cool slightly and get crunchy. Slice into quarters and serve with a small salad.

English Muffin Pizza Toast

by Suzanne (Canada)
Ingredients
One English muffin, split
2 tbsp. pizza sauce
6 pepperoni slices
2 tbsp. diced green pepper, or red
1/3 cup shredded cheese

Directions:
Split English muffin and toast under broiler, until light brown. Spread 1 T. of pizza sauce on each half of English muffin. Then add pepperoni and green pepper.
Place half of the cheese on each English muffin.
Place back under broiler until cheese is golden brown.

Liven these up by having the kids make pizza faces!

Pizza Bagels
by Teresa (Ohio)

Ingredients

Bagels, pepperoni, provolone cheese.

Directions

Half bagels and top with one slice of provolone cheese. Add 3 or 4 slices of pepperoni. Place bagels in microwave on microwave-safe plate or paper towel. Watch for cheese to begin to melt. Serve!

Pizza Bites

Ingredients
homemade pizza dough or store-bought dough
8 ounces mozzarella cheese, cut in cubes
Slices of pepperoni or pepperoni chunks
Ham chunks or ham cut up in small pieces
1/4 cup olive oil
1 teaspoon dried Italian seasoning
3 T. grated Parmesan cheese
2 Cups pasta sauce

Directions
Knead dough on a lightly floured surface and roll into a rectangle. Cut dough into small squares. Place a slice of pepperoni or ham and top with cheese. Fold dough in half and press edges together with a fork. Place on cookie sheet. In small bowl, blend together olive oil and seasoning together. With pastry brush, brush oil over pizza bites. Sprinkle with Parmesan cheese. Bake at 400 degrees for 15-18 minutes until golden brown. Serve with pasta sauce for dipping.

Pizza Crescent Rolls

Ingredients
10 oz. sliced pepperoni
1/2 Cup-1 Cup mozzarella cheese, shredded
2 (8 oz.) cans refrigerated crescent rolls

Directions
Unroll crescent dough and lay on flat surface. Add 3 slices of pepperoni onto each triangle and sprinkle with cheese. Starting with the long end, roll dough to end. Press edges to seal. Place each roll on a cookie sheet and bake at 375 degrees for 10-12 minutes until golden brown.

Zucchini Crust Pizza Pie

Ingredients
2 Cups shredded zucchini
1 tsp salt
1 egg, beaten
1 Cup mozzarella, shredded
1/4 lb. ground beef or chicken, optional
1 onion, diced
1 Cup pizza sauce
1 garlic clove, minced
1 tsp dried oregano
other pizza toppings of your choice

Directions
Spray a pie plate with cooking spray and preheat oven at 400 degrees. In a bowl, add shredded zucchini and salt together and let sit 15 minutes. Squeeze excess liquid out of zucchini and place back in empty bowl. Add egg and 1/2 Cup cheese to zucchini and stir together. Press mixture onto bottom of pie plate to make a crust. Bake for 15-20 minutes until lightly brown.
Brown beef and onion until cooked and drain off grease. Stir in pizza sauce and seasonings.
Spread sauce over zucchini crust and top with remaining cheese. Sprinkle any additional pizza toppings of your choice.
Bake an additional15 to 20 minutes or until cheese is melted.

Cauliflower Pizza Crust

Ingredients
bunch cauliflower cut in florets or 2 cups frozen
3 eggs
1/4 Cup mozzarella cheese, shredded
1 tsp basil
sprinkle of salt and pepper
pizza toppings, 1/4-1/2 Cup pizza sauce and 1/2 Cup mozzarella cheese

Directions
Steam cauliflower in microwave until tender. Mash cauliflower and allow to cool. Stir in 3 eggs and 1/4 Cup mozzarella cheese until well blended. Press mixture into a greased pie plate or baking dish. Top with pizza sauce, 1/2 Cup mozzarella cheese and pizza toppings of your choice. Bake in a 425-degree oven for 10 minutes or until cheese is melted.

White Pizza

Ingredients
homemade pizza dough
1/4 Cup Parmesan cheese
8 oz. or 1 Cup cottage cheese
1 Cup or 8 oz. mozzarella cheese, shredded
pinch Italian seasoning or mixed herbs
Pizza toppings of your choice good choices could
include diced tomatoes, sliced peppers, chopped
olives, baby spinach

Directions
Press pizza dough into pizza pan. Spread cottage
cheese, mozzarella and parmesan cheeses over
crust. Add seasoning and toppings of your choice.
Bake in a 425-degree oven for 20-25 minutes until
pizza is lightly golden brown and cheeses are melted.

Quick Pizza Crust Ideas

If you don't have time or want to make a homemade pizza crust recipe, try these options for pizza crusts.

- English muffins, split in half
- Bagels, split in half
- French Bread, cut in half lengthwise
- Pita bread
- Ready-made store-bought crust
- Tortillas

Taco Pizza

Ingredients
1 can or 1-2 Cups homemade refried beans
1/4 Cup tomato sauce
1 lb. ground beef
1-2 Tablespoons taco seasoning
pizza dough
cheddar cheese, shredded

Additional toppings to add:
chopped tomatoes
chopped olives
chopped lettuce
chopped onions
salsa or taco sauce

Directions
In a skillet, brown beef and drain. Add meat back to skillet and stir in refried beans. Blend together and stir in tomato sauce and taco seasoning. Taste and if desired add more tomato sauce and/or taco seasoning.

Allow to cool slightly. Spread pizza dough into pizza pan. Spread taco beans mixture over crust. Sprinkle with cheddar cheese. Bake for 20 minutes or until crust is browned and cheese is melted.

Layer pizza with toppings your family likes such as chopped lettuce, chopped tomatoes, chopped onions, olives and serve salsa or taco sauce on the side for those who like it.

Flatbread pizzas

by Ruth, (USA)

Ingredients

Whole wheat flatbread
Pizza sauce
Fresh basil
Fresh tomato slices
Fresh diced red pepper
Fresh chopped green onion
Shredded Italian cheese

Directions

Create pizza with listed ingredients and toast in toaster oven at 350 degrees until cheese is melted.

More Easy Pizza Ideas

Need a new idea beyond pepperoni and cheese pizza, try one of these ideas:

- Top pizza with cooked fajita chicken meat
- Make a Greek type pizza with feta cheese, chopped tomatoes, chopped cooked chicken and sliced olives
- A Mexican pizza with taco seasoned hamburger meat and taco fixings
- Barbecue chicken pizza with cheddar cheese

Pizza Snack Cups

By Ed

Ingredients

1 12oz. refrigerated biscuits or use homemade pizza dough
1/2 lb. ground beef or sausage
1 jar (14 oz.) pizza sauce
1/2 Cup shredded mozzarella cheese
sliced pepperoni, optional

Directions

Preheat oven to 375 degrees F.
Spray a 12-cup muffin tin, then evenly press the biscuit dough into the cups, bottom and up the sides. In a small skillet, brown the beef or pork over medium high heat. Drain off grease. Stir in pizza sauce and return to the stove to heat through.

Evenly spoon mixture into each of the dough cups. Top with cheese and pepperoni. Bake for 10 - 15 minutes until lightly golden brown.

Meatball Pizza

Ingredients
pkg. frozen mini meatballs
1 Cup pizza sauce
pizza dough
1-2 Cups shredded mozzarella cheese
additional toppings if desired

Directions
Preheat oven to 450°. Cook meatballs in oven until cooked through. Spread pizza crust into a pizza pan and spread sauce over crust. Sprinkle with cheese and top with mini meatballs. Add additional toppings if you'd like. Bake pizza for 10 - 15 minutes or until cheese is melted.

Pizza Quesadillas

Ingredients
8 flour tortillas
1 Cup pizza sauce
1 Cup cheddar or mozzarella cheese, shredded

Directions
Lay 4 tortillas on a griddle over low heat. Spread 1/4 Cup of sauce over each tortilla. Sprinkle each tortilla with cheese. Place a second tortilla over the top of each. Cook 5 minutes or until the bottom is lightly browned. Carefully flip the tortilla and cook an additional 3 minutes or until nicely browned. Remove and cut into triangles.

How to Make Calzones
Directions
To create calzones, roll balls of pizza dough into circles. Number of circles depends on what size you'd like them and how many you are serving.

Top half of each calzone circle with desired toppings. Fold over dough and roll edges together. Pinch seams together.

Bake at 450 degrees for 10-15 minutes.

Calzone Filling Recipes

Ham and Cheese Calzone
2 Cups diced ham or sliced pepperoni
2 Cups cheddar cheese, shredded
Parmesan cheese, optional
Dried basil, optional
Top calzone with ham and cheese and sprinkle with parmesan and basil.

Vegetable Calzone Recipe
pkg frozen spinach, thawed and drained
1 tomato, diced finely
3/4 Cup cottage cheese
3/4 Cup mozzarella cheese
salt and pepper
1 Tablespoon Italian seasoning
Sauté spinach in a frying pan and drain well. Mix ingredients together and lay on top of your calzone(s). Follow directions on how to make your calzone.

Other vegetables that would be good in a calzone:
chopped broccoli
sliced mushrooms
chopped olives
chopped onions
pesto
garlic
potato and cheese combo
sliced green or other color peppers
artichokes

Meat to add to your calzone:
cooked sausage
chopped ham
sliced pepperoni
cooked chopped or shredded chicken
ground hamburger

Chicken Calzone Recipe
shredded chicken or chicken cubed
Cook chicken. Season with salt and pepper. Stir in
any ingredients you'd like such as
spinach, shredded cheese, cooked chopped broccoli,
diced tomatoes or pesto.
My favorite chicken combo is chicken, broccoli and
cheddar cheese. Sprinkle calzone dough with
chopped cooked chicken, steamed chopped broccoli
and sprinkle with cheddar cheese. Season with Italian
seasoning or Basil and seal edges.

Cheese Calzone Recipe

1 Cup cottage or ricotta cheese

2 Cups mozzarella cheese, shredded

1/4 Cup Parmesan cheese

1 teaspoon Italian seasoning

1 teaspoon garlic powder or 1-2 cloves fresh garlic, minced

In a bowl, mix cheeses and seasonings. Add to rolled calzone dough and seal edges.

Pizza Theme Dinners

Pizza Dip

Ingredients
1/2 lb. ground beef or chicken
2 Cups pizza sauce
10 ounces mozzarella cheese, shredded
8 ounces cheddar cheese, shredded
2 loaves French bread cut in cubes
vegetables cut in sticks or slices

Directions
Brown beef and drain off grease. Stir together beef, sauce and cheeses. Add to a crock pot or fondue pot. Allow cheeses to melt and fondue to warm. Dip bread cubes and/or cut vegetables in fondue.

Pizza Meatloaf

Ingredients

1 egg
1/2 Cup pizza sauce
1/4 Cup bread crumbs, seasoned
1/2 teaspoon Italian seasoning
1 1/2 lbs. ground beef
1 1/2 Cup shredded mozzarella cheese
sliced pepperoni

Directions

In mixing bowl, combine beef, bread crumbs, egg, pizza sauce and Italian seasoning together. Place in a bread pan. Top with additional sauce, if desired.

Bake at 350 degrees for 30 minutes. Then sprinkle top with shredded mozzarella cheese and pepperoni. Continue to bake until meat is cooked through and cheese is melted.

Pizza Dogs

Ingredients
8 hot dogs
1-2 Cups pizza sauce
8 hot dog buns
1 Cup mozzarella cheese

Directions
Cook hot dogs according to package directions. Place on hot dog bun and spread pizza sauce over the top and sprinkle with cheese. Place on a cookie sheet and broil for 2 minutes until cheese melts.

Pizza Turnovers

Ingredients
pizza dough
1/4 Cup pizza sauce
Mozzarella cheese slices
Canadian bacon slices
1 T. milk
2 T. Parmesan cheese, grated

Directions
Preheat oven to 400 degrees and spray a flat baking sheet or stone with cooking spray.
Roll pizza dough onto the flat baking sheet. Cut into small squares. Spread sauce over each square except along the edges of the dough. Place a cheese slice and a slice of bacon. Fold a corner of the square to the opposite corner to form a triangle. Press the edges together with a fork to seal. Brush each turnover with milk and sprinkle the top with Parmesan cheese. Bake for 10-15 minutes until golden brown.

Pizza Burger

Ingredients

1 lb. ground beef
4 hamburger buns
1 Cup pizza sauce
1 Cup mozzarella cheese, shredded

Directions

Form beef into patties and broil or grill until cooked through. Toast hamburger buns if desired. Top each burger with pizza sauce and sprinkle with cheese. Broil for one minute or until cheese melts. Serve each burger in a toasted bun.

Pizza Soup

Ingredients
8 oz. (2 small cans) sliced mushrooms
1 Can black olives, sliced
4 Cups water
15 oz. pizza sauce or spaghetti sauce
2 Tablespoons Italian seasoning
Chopped pepperoni, chopped Canadian bacon
chopped green peppers or other favorite pizza
toppings
mozzarella cheese, shredded for topping

Directions
Mix together mushrooms, olives, water, sauce and
Italian seasoning. Add in desired pizza toppings and
simmer 15-20 minutes.

Serve with breadsticks or garlic bread on the side, if
desired.

Pizza Quiche

Ingredients
pie crust
1 Cup shredded mozzarella cheese
pepperoni chunks
ham chunks, optional
1 1/2 Cups milk
4 eggs
2 T. flour
1 tsp. basil
pinch of salt and pepper

Directions
In pie crust, sprinkle shredded cheese over the
bottom and reserve some for the top of the quiche.
Add pepperoni and ham chunks over the top of the
cheese reserving some for the top.
In a bowl, blend together eggs, flour, milk and basil.
Season with salt and pepper and pour eggs over pie
crust. Top with reserved cheese, ham and pepperoni
chunks. Bake in a 350-degree oven for 35-40 minutes
or until knife inserted in middle comes out clean.

Crockpot Pretend Pizza

Ingredients

1 1/2 lb. ground beef or ground Italian sausage
1 jar (15 oz.) pizza sauce
3 Cups fresh spinach, chopped
12 slices pepperoni
1 Cup green olives, sliced
1 Cup fresh mushrooms, sliced
1 Cup sliced onion, diced or grated
3 cups Mozzarella cheese, shredded

Directions

Cook meat until browned and drain off excess grease. Stir in pizza sauce and add half of mixture in a crockpot. Layer half of each ingredient; spinach, pepperoni, mushrooms, olives, onion and cheese. Repeat layers starting with remaining sauce. Cook on low for 4-5 hours. Allow to sit for 10-15 minutes before serving.

Chicken Mushroom Pizza

Ingredients
1 French baguette or Italian loaf
1/2 Cup pizza sauce
1 Cup pizza cheese, shredded
1 (6 oz.) pkg. Italian seasoned chicken breast strips, cooked
1 1/2 Cup mushrooms, sliced

Directions
Cut bread in half and scoop some of the insides of the bread out to make a shell. Spread sauce inside. Sprinkle with cheese. Top with chicken strips and mushrooms. Bake at 400 degrees for 15-20 minutes until cheese is melted.

Breakfast Pizza

Ingredients
1 French baguette or Italian loaf
1 Cup cheddar cheese, shredded
1 Cup ham, cooked and chopped
2 large eggs
1/2 Cup milk

Directions
Cut bread in half and scoop the insides of the bread out to make a shell.
Sprinkle shell with cheese and add chopped ham to the top. In a bowl, blend together eggs and milk until well beaten. Pour eggs inside the shell. Bake at 400 degrees for 10-15 minutes until eggs are cooked. Cut into slices before serving.

Pizza Salad

Ingredients
pkg. mixed salad greens
cherry tomatoes, sliced in half
red onion, sliced or diced small
sweet red pepper, sliced
1 (6 oz.) pkg. sliced pepperoni
1 (4 oz.) pkg. mozzarella cheese, shredded

Salad Dressing
1/2 Cup olive oil
1/3 Cup white vinegar
1 tsp parsley
1/8 tsp dried basil
1 garlic clove, minced
pinch of salt and pepper

Italian seasoned croutons, optional

Directions
In a serving bowl, layer salad greens, tomatoes, onion, red pepper, pepperoni and cheese. Toss. Combine all salad dressing ingredients together. Add pour over salad before serving. Top with croutons, if desired.

Dessert Pizzas

Cookie Pizza

Ingredients
1/2 Cup butter softened
1 Cup powdered sugar
1 egg
1/4 Cup milk
1/2 teaspoon vanilla extract
1/2 teaspoon almond or lemon extract
2 1/2 Cups flour
1 teaspoon baking soda
1/2 teaspoon cream of tartar

Toppings:
sliced fruit
cream cheese or vanilla frosting

Directions
In a mixer cream together, butter and sugar. Then add in egg, milk and extracts. Add flour, baking soda and cream tartar and blend together until forms a soft dough.
Grease a pizza pan and roll out cookie dough to fit the pan. Or make individual pizzas by rolling out dough and then cutting out with round cookie cutters.
Bake at 375 degrees for 7-9 minutes or until lightly, golden brown.

Once cookies have cooled off, spread frosting over the top of the cookies and arrange cut fruit over the top of the fruit pizzas.

Brownie Pizza

Directions

This is like the cookie pizza but instead of using sugar cookie dough for the crust, spread brownie batter into the bottom of the pizza pan. Bake. Then frost and top with sliced fruit.

43683217R00031

Made in the USA
Middletown, DE
27 April 2019